WHY WE FAIL AT ROMANTIC RELATIONSHIPS

GEORGE BISSETT

DEDICATION

This book is dedicated to my sister, Connie Abbott and my brother, Monty - two really good people who always made their families their number one priority. Unfortunately, Monty died last year and, along with his own family, I miss him every day, and know that Connie does, too.

Both of my siblings somehow knew things I really never got - such as how to maintain strong and loving connections and how to be unselfish with their time.

The world would be a much better place if everyone in it was like Connie and Monty.

ACKNOWLEDGEMENTS

Thanks to Bob and Dawn Bray, two friends who acted as a sounding board for me while I was writing this book. The material contained herein was gleaned from an informal document that I used as a guide for workshops on this topic.

Christina (Chrissy) Rice, is the person who read and edited this material and converted it into the various "e-book" languages that I know absolutely nothing about. Thank heaven she does.

TABLE OF CONTENTS

INTRODUCTION

According to my friend and business partner, Bob Bray, it is important to clarify that this book is NOT about sex. At least that's not the primary focus. It is about romance - mostly because, without romance, sex can become less than it could/should be.

I disagree with those who believe that love and sex should be intrinsically linked at all times when, to me, love and sex seem to be separate entities. But that is just my opinion and whatever your opinion is, it is every bit as valid as mine.

With that explanation down and done I felt kind of lyrical so I have inserted, below, my very own attempt at poetic verse.

Romantic Relationships are rare

Coveted by many

Experienced by few

And the many accept the love

We believe we deserve

When I made the decision to write this book the idea I had in mind seemed so clear but as soon as I put pen to paper (okay, so it was finger to keyboard) things changed... well, they changed after pecking out a couple thousand words, but still...

The first draft went right into talking about change and then I thought that there should be a discussion on how we think and why we think the way we do – and that's important because thoughts lead to actions and feelings. Or, what we think determines how we act and how we feel.

As always, Bob did a read-through of the rough draft and politely commented that my effort at lyrical writing would not win any awards. He also noted that the proper name for my offering is "prose poem" because it plants one foot in prose, the other in poetry, both heels resting precariously on banana peels.

The next suggestion from Bob was that I should expand the sections on codependency and counter dependency so as to make them more understandable to those readers who may not have studied or researched those behaviors. The sad part is that most relationships of codependency and/or counter dependency are very stressful.

MANAGING RELATIONSHIP STRESS

Many things that are stressful to us as a result of the behaviors of others can be handled if one is able to detach. The definition of detachment is summed up by the following:

- I didn't cause it.

- I can't control it.

- I can't cure it.

- I can't change it – but I can change myself.

If you can accept and adopt the foregoing information you will be on the path to no longer suffering as a result of someone else's behavior because you are what your deep driving desire is. As your desire is, so is your will. As your will is, so is your deed. As your deed is, so is your destiny. Or, another way of saying it is, if you don't know where you're going any road will get you there.

The title, "Why We Fail At Romantic Relationships", was chosen because I wanted to talk about putting the romance back into intimate relationships so that the sexual part becomes a reward and not a duty or a punishment.

Let me explain...

Sexual intercourse can obviously be used for procreation but it can also be used to communicate, to comfort, and - unfortunately - to punish. Same act with different reasons and outcomes.

Huh! Being a human can be mind-bending at times.

LET'S LOOK AT A DEFINITION:

Romantic love is when the chemicals in your brain kick in and you feel an emotional high, exhilaration, passion, and elation when you and your lover are together.

The old saying about love being blind truly describes romantic love. Many who are in the midst of romantic love want to be with their lover all the time and can overlook faults, conflict, and abuse. Those couples would probably agree that, if Love doesn't actually make the world go around it certainly makes the trip enjoyable and interesting. Much better than whatever's in second spot.

During the initial stages of a romantic relationship, there is more often more emphasis on emotions — especially those of love, intimacy, compassion, appreciation, and affinity — rather than physical intimacy. Romantic love in the early stages is often characterized by uncertainty, along with emotional anxiety that love may not be returned.

Romance is personal. To be romantic, you must be personal and do personal kind of things. A romantic relationship is one where both people feel that little quiver inside when the other enters the room. **Romance** is the expressive and pleasurable feeling from an emotional attraction towards another person associated with love.

Infatuation is an aspect of romantic love but most individuals cannot sustain that type of emotional high for an extended period of time – such as years and years. The infatuation period is also referred to as honeymoon phase, puppy love, sexual love, having a crush, infatuation, limerence – which is an involuntary state of mind caused by a romantic attraction to another person *combined* with an overwhelming, obsessive need to have one's feelings reciprocated.

A person will realize that the infatuation/romantic love phase of their relationship is declining or wearing off when a sense of disillusionment sets in. Spouses may become more critical of one another, become easily irritated at things that didn't bother them earlier in their relationship, have less patience with each other, and could be indifferent to the wants and feelings of each other. Not bailing out and communicating dreams, desires, thoughts, and feelings with one another can lead to the wonderful stage of mature love.

In the context of romantic love relationships, romance usually implies an expression of one's strong romantic love, or one's deep and strong emotional desires to connect with another person intimately or romantically. Historically, the term *"romance"* originates with the medieval ideal of chivalry as set out in its *Romance* literature.

Humans have a natural inclination to form bonds with one another through social interactions, be it through verbal communication or nonverbal gestures. With some individuals, these social interactions can span beyond what one would typically view as a platonic relationship. Positive romantic relationships are a crucial part of society in that not only do these relations affect those that are in participation, but they can also have an influence on those that are in close vicinity.

Sometimes, what may be viewed as tradition does not allow for as much of a range that is realistically present among those that are aiming for a healthy positive relationship. Some traditional approaches place certain responsibilities or unsaid assumptions on each party, where each person is expected to act a certain way simply because that's how it's supposed to be. With positive psychology – an approach to help humans prosper and lead healthy, happy lives – there seems to be a push for a more equal division of responsibilities regardless of sex, gender, or any other circumstances. Each individual can learn about love on more than one level; there is an acknowledgment of the word having multiple meanings, as well as relationships having multiple outcomes, as a result of previous attachment patterns in other social domains (i.e. parenting).

RELATIONSHIPS OF CODEPENDENCE

Relationships of Codependence are dysfunctional relationships - relationships that do not work to meet our needs. That does not mean just romantic relationships, or family relationships, or even human relationships in general.

Co-dependency is a learned behavior that can be passed down from one generation to another. It is an emotional and behavioral condition that affects an individual's ability to have a healthy, mutually satisfying relationship. It is also known as "relationship addiction" because people with codependency often form or maintain relationships that are one-sided, emotionally destructive and/or abusive. The disorder was identified following years of studying interpersonal relationships in families of alcoholics.

Co-dependent behavior is learned by watching and imitating other family members or people of influence who display this type of behavior. It can affect a parent, spouse, child, co-worker who has grown up in some form of dysfunction. This could be from the affects of abuse, addiction, separation or divorce. Even people who have grown up in a relatively stable environment can be affected by parents overworking or not spending time generally with children, giving the subtle message, "I am not okay".

There are generally thought to be three types of codependents:

1. Caretakers: relate to others primarily through roles that put them in a position of the giver, helper, supporter, and nurturer, etc. "Everyone's needs are more important than my own."

2. Romance/relationship addiction: must be in a "relationship" and be "special" to someone in order to be okay with oneself; may use caretaking and sexuality to gain approval/acceptance; goes from relationship to relationship. "You're no one unless someone loves you."

3. Messiah complex: savior of the family, church, world; over-responsible, doesn't ask for help, and tries to make self-indispensable. "If I don't do it, it won't get done.

The general symptoms of codependency include:

- External-reference on other person or people.

- Tries to control behavior of others through approval-seeking and people-pleasing behavior.

- Experiences intimacy by discounting own feelings, and empathizing with feelings of others.

- Loss of healthy boundaries, generally resulting from doing things for others that violate one's values, and from accepting unacceptable behavior from others.

- Frozen feelings, numbness with regard to one's own feelings. Depression may also result from repressed anger.

- Low self-esteem. Self is valued according to others' opinions. Uses martyr, victim, and messiah role to bolster self-esteem.

- Generalized anxiety, related to lack of control of one's life.

- Mental preoccupation. Racing thoughts. Inability to enjoy mental silence and serenity.

- Lack of assertiveness: inability to ask directly for one's true needs. Inability to confront unhealthy behavior in others.

- Narcissism. In the absence of healthy, legitimate boundaries, others are seen as for or against self.

Co-dependency is an umbrella term for a range of issues that can result from the affliction. Codependency is an emotional, behavioral, and psychological pattern of coping which develops as a result of prolonged exposure to and practice of a dysfunctional set of family rules. In turn, these rules make difficult or impossible for the open expression of thoughts and feelings. Normal identity development is thereby interrupted; codependency is the reflection of a delayed identity development. In order to make healthy changes for yourself, one must be ready to take action against his/her current behaviors. Long-term remediation of codependency requires the identification of dysfunctional coping strategies that have persisted from childhood, as well as the recognition and acceptance of healthier choices.

The fact that dysfunction exists in our romantic, family, and human relationships is a symptom of the dysfunction that exists in our relationship with life - with being human. It is a symptom of the dysfunction which exists in our relationships with ourselves as human beings.

And the dysfunction that exists in our relationship with ourselves is a symptom of behavioral unbalance, of not being in balance and harmony, of feeling 'disconnected'.

That is why it is so important to enlarge our perspective, to look beyond the romantic relationship in which we are having problems. It is important to look beyond the dysfunction that exists in our relationships with other people.

The surest way to bring people into your circle (closer to you) may be to attract them in through behavior changes. If you decide to look at your behaviors with an eye to change, one way to make it easier to accept is to measure it against your Best Interest, which is defined as not being deliberately hurtful or harmful to self or others. In order to understand it more fully – at least from my perspective – when I apply the principle of Best Interest before I do whatever I am intending to do I can be satisfied that I am doing 'it' to help me and not to hurt others. But, I have no control over how other may see my actions.

Let that sink in…

My Best Interest is served when my plans and/or actions are not intended to be deliberately hurtful or harmful to myself or others. Others may CHOOSE to feel hurt but that is none of my business.

WHY WE FAIL AT ROMANTIC RELATIONSHIPS

The more you enlarge your perspective, the closer you will get to the cause instead of just dealing with the symptoms. For example, the more you look at the dysfunction in your relationship with yourself as a human being the more you can understand the dysfunction in your romantic relationship(s). As long as you believe that you have to have an *other* in your life to be happy, you are really just an addict trying to protect your supply - using another person as your drug of choice. That is not a good thing, nor is it a loving thing.

If we humans fail to get our romantic needs met it is usually because we do not really know who we are and why we are here, and we have not investigated our values and beliefs about the meaning and purpose of our lives. This investigation is important because our human values and beliefs determine how we see the world – our perspective on the world around us. And human personalities are a reflection of our individual perspectives, which will dictate our long-term success with relationships – especially Romantic Relationships.

This is important because we cannot deny our values and beliefs. Most of our relationship failures come about when we present ourselves as someone or something we are not and we maintain the charade through conscious application of willpower. Eventually we may become overtired and our willpower will fail and our true self takes over. That is when calm becomes angry, reasonable becomes unreasonable, and dependable becomes undependable.

And that's what makes Romantic Relationships so very complex – so let's look at what drives us as human beings.

Our Five Basic Needs

In psychology, it is assumed that people have certain basic needs and in our Dynamic Discovery program they are classified under five headings for which we apply the acronym LAFFS:

1) Love & Belonging - this includes sex, families or loved ones as well as groups.

2) Achievement, Power and Recognition – which includes feeling worthwhile as well as winning.

3) Freedom - includes independence, autonomy, and your own 'space'.

4) Fun - includes pleasure and enjoyment.

5) Survival - includes nourishment and shelter,

Whether we are aware of it or not, we are all the time acting to meet these needs, but we don't necessarily act effectively. Socializing with people is an effective way to meet our need for belonging while isolating and self-pitying in the hope that people will come to us is generally an ineffective way of meeting that need; it is painful and costly (in psychological terms) and seems to never work in the long term.

So if life is unsatisfactory or we are distressed or in trouble, one basic thing to check is whether we are succeeding in meeting our four (4) basic psychological needs (LAAF) – only those 4 because the 5th, survival, is implied – because it is in how we meet those 4 'psychological' needs that we run into trouble.

RELATIONSHIP MAPS

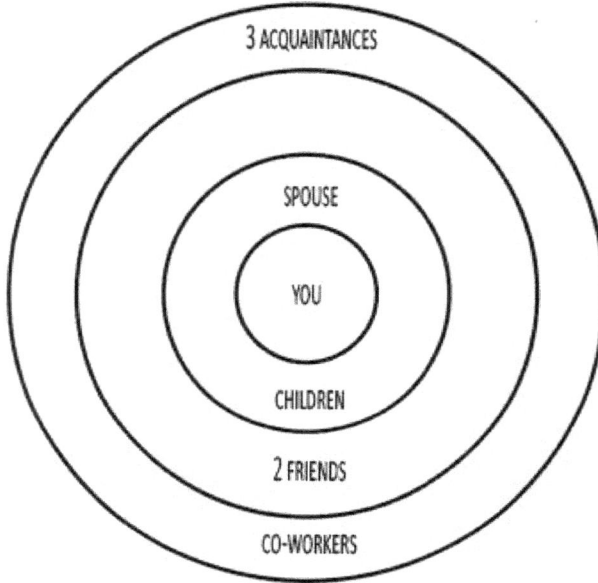

The relationship map above is an example of one client's 'Ideal World', where she <u>wanted</u> to feel closest to her own family (first ring) and then to friends (second ring) and lastly acquaintances and co-workers. Unfortunately, her actual map was quite different because (as she said) her problems drove her family away – although they would say that she withdrew from them. Because of the confusion of her loneliness, she had become resentful toward those whom she thought were not appreciative of, or caring for her – that somehow <u>they</u> should have been able to resolve <u>her</u> problems. In time, she felt closer to strangers than to family and friends because there was no attachment and therefore no emotional risk. But, there was a downside: There were no feelings of love and belonging but lots of emptiness and loneliness. Lots.

Once this person started working on her recovery, the task that was created for her was to self-evaluate for how <u>her</u> thoughts and actions created the feelings in her that made her withdraw and thereby become even more lonely and then resentful. By honestly looking at her part in the situation and then applying the principles of Best Interest to her intended actions she could ensure that her intention was to help herself, not to hurt others.

Stop reading and close your eyes down and take a moment to see if you can visualize how you can serve your Best Interest by doing things to help yourself and not to hurt others. Even if there are others who <u>choose</u> to feel and act hurt.

So, is what you're doing helping your situation or hurting it? Think about your answer: Helping _____   Hurting _____

Use the empty circles below to chart your <u>actual</u> relationship map.

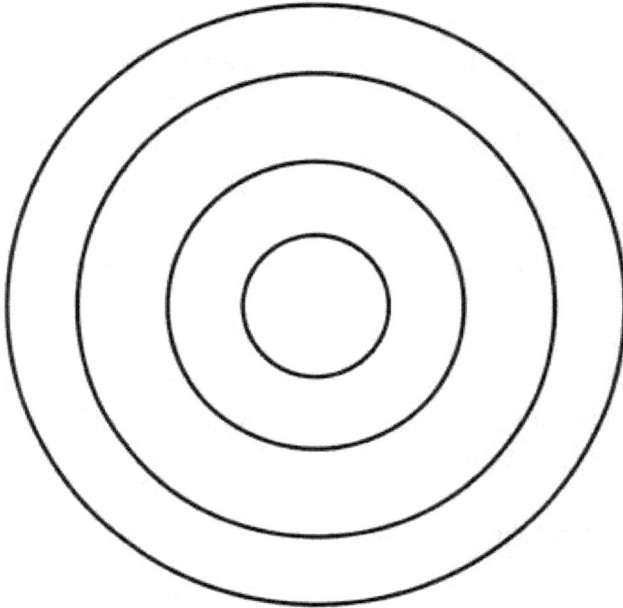

If you can honestly answer that your actions meet the principles of Best Interest then the fact that others may <u>choose</u> to feel hurt is not your problem.

Based upon what you charted in the above circles you should answer some questions:

- What things have you done to try to resolve your problems? _____

- How did it work out?

_____

- Did it help you get what you want?

  _____

- What do you want?

  _____

- If you got that, what would it mean to you?

  _____

- How do you feel about the people in your life?

  _____

- How would you prefer to be feeling?

  _____

- What have you been thinking that you don't like? Or, has not helped you get what you want?

  _____

- If this is what you are thinking, how would you expect to feel?

  _____

- If you were happy, what would you be thinking?

  _____

- What could you do to start thinking that way?

  _____

- What have you been doing that you do not like doing? Or has not helped you get what you want?

  _____

- What would you prefer to be doing?

  _____

- How has your behavior affected your relationships?

  _____

- What are your best interests, and where are you in relation to them?

  _____

Use the space below to self-evaluate the relationship between your current behaviors and your best interests.

_____

_____

_____

_____

_____

_____

_____

_____

_____

_____

_____

_____

INHERITED CHILDISH SHAME

The values and beliefs we learn as children - the repression and distortion of our emotional process in reaction to the attitudes and behavior patterns we adopt to survive in an emotionally repressive, hostile environment - create the shame we suffer from as adults. That shame is toxic and never was our own. Never! If we could only see that shame without the emotion that goes along with it, we would be able to see that we did nothing to be ashamed of. Kids have little or no power and learn from the world around them – whether what they learn is helpful or hurtful. Just as everyone else does. Just as it was for our parents when they were little kids and were wounded and shamed. Just as it was for their parents before them… and so on.

So the shame we learn has been passed down from generation to generation – whether it is passed down through our immediate family or other families. Kids are emotional sponges, soaking up whatever it is they see and hear. And to make it even more complicated, we may learn <u>how</u> to do something from what we've seen or heard or <u>how not</u> to do that same thing.

There must be no blame here as blame does not solve problems. For the most part, the people we usually blame are not 'bad guys'; they are usually people who themselves have wounded souls, broken hearts, and/or scrambled minds.

If we are reacting out of what our emotional truth was when we were five or nine or fourteen, then we are not capable of responding appropriately to what is happening in the moment; we are not being in the present. When our behaviors are based on attitudes and beliefs that are false or distorted, then our feelings cannot be trusted. When we are acting out of our childhood emotional wounds, then what we are feeling may have very little to do with the situation we are in or with the people with whom we are dealing in the moment. In order to be present in the moment in a healthy, age-appropriate way it is necessary to deal with our unwanted thoughts, feelings and actions. The behaviors we need to change are the behaviors that have been running our lives because we have been unconsciously reacting to life out of the emotional wounds and attitudes, the old behaviors we learned in our childhoods.

CODEPENDENCE

Consider this: Codependence is a behavior of reaction.

As long as we are reacting codependently we are being a victim. We are not owning our power if we are reacting. Many of us have reacted to being hurt in our romantic relationships by going to the other extreme - overreacting to the point where we spent many years out of romantic relationships. Then we try a romantic relationship again and have another disaster because we are reacting to our childhood behavioral programming and we again react to our reaction by overreacting to the other extreme.

THE KEY IS TO KNOW WHAT WE *WANT*

It is not usual to think in terms of meeting our Love and Belonging needs each day as we are more likely to wonder whether a friend would be able to meet us for lunch or to consider getting a group together for a social evening. We may want to meet a friend or mingle with a group or want 'our' football team or 'our' political party to win.

What usually drives us as social beings is our wants since we don't think of our needs as such. We think of what we want, behave to get what we want, fantasize about what we want and so on. We can check whether we are meeting our wants and needs through addressing three basic questions:

1. What do I want?

   _____

   _____

2. What am I doing to get what I want?

   _____

   _____

3. Is it working?

   _____

   _____

PLANNING

In order to get what we want, we need to make a plan that is workable, meaning that it is a plan we can successfully implement - in other words, it concentrates on the things that are in our control to do:

- You may not be able to make your spouse talk to you but you can talk to your spouse.

- You may not be able to make your teenage son treat you with respect but you can decide that you will no longer provide a laundry and catering service to a son who treats you with contempt.

- You may not be able to make the company give you a promotion but you can look for a promotion, lobby for it and apply for the job when it comes up.

In this way, we are empowered by focusing on the power of doing what is in our control to do.

DOING

Emotions are a wonderful, immediate and 'alive' source of information about how we are doing and whether we are happy with what is going on in our lives. But it is very, very hard to change our emotions directly. It is easier to change our thinking: to decide, for example, that we will no longer think of ourselves as victims or to decide that in our thoughts we will concentrate on what we can do rather than what we think everybody else ought to do.

Changing what we do is the key to changing

how we feel and to getting what we want.

Sometimes we are so caught up in anger, depression or resentment that even changing how we think seems an impossible task - in such situations a positive change in what we <u>do</u> may be the best we can manage.

CONTROL

The issue of control is also of great importance.

As part of meeting our needs we need control: one person seeks control through position and money; another wants to control his or her physical space, like the teenager who bans all parents and parent-like persons from her room; another wants to chair the committee; another wants an office with a corner and two windows; another wants a specific meal on the table at precisely 6.30 pm.

Control gets us into trouble in two primary ways: when we try to control other people, and when we use drugs and alcohol to give us a false sense of control. At the very heart is the idea that the only person I can really control is myself. If I think I can control others I am moving in the direction of frustration. If I think others can control me (and so are to blame for all that goes on in my life) I tend to do nothing and again head for frustration.

There may indeed be things that 'happen' to us and for which we are not personally responsible but we can choose what we do about these things. Trying to control other people is a losing game; a never-ending battle that alienates us from others and causes endless pain and frustration.

This is why it is vital to stick to what is in our own control to do and to respect the right of other people to meet their own needs in their own way.

We can, of course, get an instant sense of control from alcohol and some other drugs. Unfortunately, our lives are never more <u>out of control</u> than when we are drunk or drugged. There are very few people in this world who ever woke up with a hangover to find that they had fewer problems than they had when they started using the night before.

Excessive drinking and the use of drugs have to be replaced by doing something else - and that something else has to have a fair chance of getting us what we want in life.

THE SOLUTION
(IS IN THE PRESENT AND THE FUTURE)

Counselling is often thought to involve delving into the past. In Dynamic Discovery we also visit the past but to a much lesser extent than those who use other approaches - this is not a criticism of those other approaches, it is simply a way in which Dynamic Discovery is different.

In Dynamic Discovery the past is seen as the source of our wants and of our ways of behaving.

Not only are the bad things that happened to you there but your successes are there too. Your focus is directed so as to learn what needs to be learned about the past but to move as quickly as feasible to becoming empowered to satisfy your needs and wants in the present and in the future because it is your present perceptions that influence your present behavior and so it is these perceptions that the Dynamic Discovery self-evaluation process will help you to work on replacing unwanted behaviours with wanted behaviours.

Understand this...

Dynamic Discovery is very much a program of hope, based on the conviction that we are products of the past but we do not have to go on being its victims.

In Dynamic Discovery we work on getting the pendulum swing to become smaller and smaller - finding the middle ground, the place of balance. Overreacting to our patterns is just as dysfunctional as reacting to the wounds that caused the patterns.

If, while we're evaluating our past, we discover a pattern - say, that we leave relationships before we can be left - and we overreact and decide to stick it out in the next relationship no matter what, that can lead to us accepting a lot of abuse in the name of recovery. If we are in reaction and trying to figure out what is right and wrong, we are giving power to the old behaviors. There are no mistakes, only lessons - which are painful but not that painful if we are not judging and shaming ourselves. What makes lessons so painful is the shame attached to it and the shame creates fear about getting hurt until we are terrified of being hurt - but what is so painful about being hurt is the shame that will beat us up after we get hurt. The hurt itself passes while the shame and judgment abuses us with is what is most painful. And often for a very long time.

We are programmed to believe that making a mistake is horribly shameful. We are programmed to believe that if we do not find happily-ever-after in a romantic relationship then we have made a mistake, or something is wrong with us. When a relationship doesn't work out we torture ourselves with recriminations about what we did wrong – or what is wrong – with us. We berate ourselves for the shame of failing. Romantic Relationships are part of our life-lessons, not the place we find happily ever after. Life is a journey, not a destination. The goal of healing is not to become perfect, it is not to get healed. Healing is a process, not a destination - we are not going to arrive at a place in this lifetime where we are completely healed.

The goal here is to make life an easier and more enjoyable experience while we are healing. The goal is to live well. To be able to feel happy, joyous, and free in the moment, the majority of the time. To get to a place where we are free to be happy in the moment most of the time, we need to change our perspectives enough to start recognizing truth when we see or hear it. And the truth is that we are just people having a human experience that is unfolding perfectly and always has been, there are no accidents, coincidences, or mistakes - so there is no blame to be assessed.

The goal here is to be our human selves and enjoy it – but we can't do that if we are judging and shaming ourselves. We can't do that if we are blaming ourselves or others.

We must start recognizing that Codependence is a choice we made when we did not know we had a choice – which means we did not have one. If we never knew how to say no, then we never really said yes. We were powerless to do anything any different than we did it. We were doing the best we knew how with the tools that we had. None of us had the power to write a different script for our lives. We need to learn from the past… and then get past it.

We need to get past the ways in which we abandoned and abused ourselves. We need to get past the ways we deprived ourselves.

We need to own that sadness before we move away from it. But we also need to stop blaming ourselves for it. It was not our fault! We did not have the power to do it any differently. It is when we start understanding the cause and effect

28

relationship between what happened to the child that we were, and the effect it had on the adult we became, that we can truly start to forgive ourselves. It is only when we start understanding on an emotional level, on a gut level, that we were powerless to do anything any differently than we did that we can truly start to accept and love ourselves for who we really are.

The hardest thing for any of us to do is to have compassion for ourselves. As children we felt responsible for the things that happened to us. We blamed ourselves for the things that were done to us and for the deprivations we suffered. There is nothing more powerful in this transformational process than being able to self-evaluate for our unwanted thoughts, feelings and actions in order to create a list of wanted thoughts, feelings and actions and then to 'see' the difference through our adult eyes. As an adult we know we have the power to say, *"It wasn't my fault. I didn't do anything wrong, I was just a little kid,"* and then acknowledge and honor the child we once were so as to love the person we are now becoming.

We can own our experiences as a child and acknowledging the reality of that child's feelings but we cannot erase the past and what happened and what we felt then. We can, however, diminish its impact upon us today and stop allowing the past to dictate our present. By releasing the emotional grief-energy that we are still carrying around we place the past where it belongs; in the past.

Take a moment to absorb this:

- What happened in the past was not your fault.

- Children only do what they are taught to do.

LIVING IN THE PRESENT

It is very important to forgive ourselves and to use that forgiveness to change our relationship with our self. We cannot love someone else in a healthy way until we learn to love ourselves - and we cannot love our self without owning all of the parts of us.

When we say that we cannot truly love others unless we love ourselves, that does not mean that we have to completely love ourselves first before we can <u>start</u> to love others. The way the process works is that every time we learn to love and accept ourselves a little bit more, we also gain the capacity to love and accept others a little bit more.

We can use our adult self to set a boundary to stop the shame and judgment so that we can find some balance – which is to not overreact or under-react out of our fear of overreacting.

The process of learning how to set internal boundaries that are in our own Best Interest is a powerful method for learning to love ourselves. Once we start loving, honoring, and respecting our self then we have a chance to be available in a healthy way for a loving Romantic Relationship.

We cannot learn to love ourselves and be at peace within until we stop judging and shaming ourselves for being human and stop fighting our own emotional process, until we stop waging war on ourselves.

If taking care of yourself causes conflict with your spouse then you may need to take another look at the relationship - either by yourself or hopefully with him/her to see if the conflict can be mediated since setting boundaries in a relationship is about 95% negotiation. Boundaries for the most part aren't rigid but some are; for instance, it is not okay to hit your spouse or call them certain names or cheat on them; things like that. Most boundaries are a matter of negotiation, which of course involves communication.

As previously mentioned, communication is really difficult. Because we all behave in ways that we learned when we were young and impressionable it is not uncommon to believe that it is shameful to be wrong or make a mistake. Too often in relationships the attempts at communication end up as a power struggle between who is right and who is wrong. One person takes the others feedback as an attack and then attacks back.

Again the wrong question is being asked because an intimate relationship is a partnership, an alliance, not some game with winners and losers. When the interaction in an intimate relationship becomes a power struggle about who is right and who is wrong then there are no winners.

Consider this: Would you sooner be right or happy?

To answer that, close your eyes down and take a moment to think back to the last dispute or argument you had with your partner and see if you can visualize whether you were trying to be right or happy. And then imagine what you might have done different to make for a more positive outcome.

We need to work in our Best Interest in order to be able to

stop reacting out of our wounds and our shame. And our Best Interest is served when our plans and/or actions are not intended to be deliberately hurtful or harmful to myself or others. Once we build a library of Best Interest activities and events that will help us feel better about ourselves we can then trust our *"smart system"* to evaluate for our needs and determining what to do in order to meet those needs and choose the best option(s). Because no other person can live my life for me, it follows that I am the one person on this planet who can restore my own dignity and self-respect. No one else can do that for me.

Let that sink in…

Do things to help yourself, not to hurt others. Others may choose to feel hurt but that is none of your business.

DISHONESTY VS INTIMACY

Many of us are taught to repress and distort our emotional process. We are trained to be emotionally dishonest when we are children. Our traditional cultural concepts of what a man is, of what a woman is, are twisted, distorted, almost comically bloated stereotypes of what masculine and feminine really are.

Many of us are set up to be emotionally dysfunctional by our interactions with others because our values and beliefs are created by what we learn from our culture, religion, and authority figures. And our values and beliefs create our personality and our personality creates our perspective and our perspective is how we see the world. To quote Anais Nin, *"We don't see the world as it is, we see it as we are."*

Your perception truly is (and must be) your reality.

What we see depends upon who we are. If we expect people to be mean and untrustworthy then, to us, that will appear to be true. That is why six eyewitnesses to an accident or crime will usually provide six different accounts – and no one is lying.

ONCE YOU KNOW HOW YOU THINK, AND WHY YOU THINK THE WAY YOU DO, IT IS POSSIBLE TO <u>CHANGE</u> THE WAY YOU THINK. YOU MIGHT WELL ASK, *"WHY WOULD I WANT TO CHANGE THE WAY I THINK?"* AND THE ANSWER IS SIMPLY THIS; IF YOU ARE NOT GETTING WHAT YOU WANT (FROM YOUR LIFE) THEN YOU WILL HAVE TO CHANGE WHAT YOU ARE DOING, FOR WE ALL KNOW THAT DOING THE SAME

THING OVER AND OVER AND EXPECTING A DIFFERENT RESULT IS INSANITY!

You can change a belief through identifying a preferred belief and adopting it through repetition. But, if you want to change anything, you must do something different. It doesn't matter whether the change is to a belief, a human behavior, or a recipe for pound cake. Doing something different will produce a change to the outcome. And behavior change starts with changing your thoughts and actions – and that will lead to a change in how you feel.

THE HEALING PROCESS

A vital part of a healing process is finding some balance in our relationship with the masculine and feminine energy within us, and achieving some balance in our relationships with the masculine and feminine energy all around us.

We cannot do that if we have twisted, distorted beliefs about the nature of masculine and feminine.

For some people, a long-term relationship may be one or two years because of their particular terror of intimacy. For these people to get into recovery they need to realize that for them to set boundaries or get angry in a Romantic Relationship might feel like they are acting like some hated authority figure from their past; someone that they had hated so much and vowed they would never be like. So they have to learn to know that it is okay to say *No* and to set boundaries in any relationship and that it doesn't mean they're being a perpetrator.

When in doubt, apply the Best Interest rule: your Best Interest is served when your plans and/or actions are not intended to be deliberately hurtful or harmful to yourself or others. Do things to help yourself, not to hurt others.

Think about that for a moment – it's in your own Best Interest to help yourself without intentionally hurting others. Those others may choose to feel hurt but that is their choice and none of your business. You have no control over how others manage their lives.

If you want to learn more about this you can download our Dynamic Discovery e-book.

We learn who we are as emotional beings from the role-modeling of our authority figures... our parents and all the other people around us – younger, older, male or female. Anyone we can learn from no matter whether the lesson is positive, negative, or neutral.

There are people in our society who have never had an emotionally honest male role model in their life. They have to become their own role model for what emotional honesty looks like in a man. And romance means nothing without emotional intimacy.

As long as we can't be emotionally romantic with ourselves, we are incapable of being emotionally romantic with another human being. It is absolutely vital to learn how to be emotionally honest with ourselves in order to share our self with another being.

It is impossible to have a truly successful Romantic Relationship without emotional honesty, which is when we are in balance and have harmony between the physical, emotional, mental, and spiritual levels of being. It is a feeling of being comfortable in our own skin, accepting of our specific position in life, and generally feeling happy and optimistic

Wow! Now that's a feeling never to be forgotten.

SEX

Sex can ultimately be an empty, barren animal coupling - involving physical pleasure but really having little to do with love - without emotional and spiritual connections.

This results in one of the major problem areas of many relationships. Without emotional intimacy many women get turned off and withhold sex because their emotional needs aren't being met - and men get angry because they don't even have a clue of what women are asking for.

What a set up! It is not women's fault.

It is also not men's fault.

It is a set up.

In our society, women are usually taught to be codependent - that is to take their self-definition and self-worth from their relationships with men, while men have been taught to be codependent on their financial success and success in their career or job. Not many of those men are taught how to be successful as husbands and fathers. Even though that has changed somewhat in the past twenty or thirty years, it is still part of the reason that women have more of a tendency to sell their souls for relationships than men do.

So it has been a double set up for women in this society for a very long time. What a shame.

HEALING

A vital part of a healing process is finding some balance in our relationship with the masculine and feminine energy within us, and achieving some balance in our relationships with the masculine and feminine energy all around us.

First of all, in our society the men were taught that it was not manly to be emotional and that what makes them successful as a man is what they produce – and then women were taught that they needed to be successful in romantic relationships with emotionally unavailable men in order to be successful as a woman.

How dumb is that?

One of the damaging concepts that many of us were taught as a child is that we are not allowed to be angry at someone we love. Many parents have told their children, "I can't be angry at you, I love you," then they continue to live their life with a partner whose only emotion is anger and who rages all the time …which makes a very sad statement. If we cannot be angry at someone we cannot be emotionally romantic with that person. Any friend who I cannot get angry at (or vice versa) and then at some later point communicate with and work through whatever the issue is, is not really a friend. It's very important to learn how to fight fair in a Romantic Relationship since some of us learned as impressionable children that if we stood up for ourself our partner would go away.

It is important to learn to fight fair without saying those really hurtful things that can't be taken back. It is also important to learn that we can stand up for ourselves and fight fair even when the other person does not fight fair. But unless we can express our anger - as well as our hurt, fear, and sadness - to another person we cannot be emotionally romantic with them. It can be wonderfully magical in a relationship when both people are in recovery and working on healing their childhood wounds.

Consider this:

An argument over one of the stupid, seemingly meaningless things that couples often argue about can turn into a mutual grieving session. Talk about an opportunity for powerful intimacy.

<u>Imagine this</u>: A fight starts and just as angry words are exchanged – or after some time has passed, or after a time out that has been structured into the relationship – one partner says to the other, "How old are your feeling right now?" and the answer is something like, "I feel about 7." The other might say, "What happened when you were 7?" and so on until the partners end up figuring out that the tone of voice one person used pushed a button about how Mom or Dad or someone else used to talk to them in a way that made them feel stupid - and when the first person reacted to that it pushed a button for the other person about how someone used to do… *whatever*. And so on. Until you both get to cry for the ways you were abused or discounted or invalidated.

It is very important to know that the Universe works on the principle of cause and effect: Our reactions do not come out of the blue; they have a cause.

What we need to learn to do is stop reacting to the long-ago past. And we can do that by tracking down the cause instead of getting all tied up in the symptom of whatever started the argument. It is dysfunctional to react from our long-ago past because that reaction is only a little bit about what is happening now.

Uncovering the "how" and "why" of our inappropriate and hurtful behaviors may be the most powerful, meaningful, traumatic, painful, explosive, heart wrenching single topic for most people.

For many of us, our hearts have been broken because we were taught to do the Dance of Love in a dysfunctional way and to the wrong music. And now they have been broken again.

If you feel pain from that statement, find a quiet and private place and, with your eyes closed, take some deep breaths and visualize breathing in a sense of wellness and calm and breathing out any of the unwanted feelings residing within you, which will break up and release some of the trapped grief energy, and, embrace that sense of wellness and calm. Repeat this exercise as many times as necessary for your body to let go of the pain and hurt.

If you cannot own, feel, and release some emotional pain energy in relating to the truth of that statement, it could mean that you don't feel safe to be emotionally honest in this moment, or that you don't feel safe to be emotionally honest with yourself in regard to this topic. And that would be a sad commentary on how much you have had to shut down your heart, how closed off you have had to become to the emotional truth of how painful being human in a dysfunctional, emotionally dishonest, spiritually hostile, love retarded cultural environment has been.

In order to completely let go of the pain and hurt, you have to work out what you really want but most people have never really thought about what they want, what they might be capable of, because they are so focused on the daily routine that they just don't take the time to think about their own future. And not knowing what you want is the route to a wasted life.

Suppose somebody said you could have or do anything you wanted in the world, anything at all, in order for you to be free of all your pain and hurt, how would you know what to choose? Not sure? Well, we have an exercise for that.

Find a private spot where you can sit quietly and, with your eyes closed, imagine that someone you really trust has just told you that you could be comfortable, content, and joyously free of your hurt and pain and then asked, "What could you do to achieve that if you knew you could not fail?"

Think about what would happen if you actually succeeded at what your answer was. Most people doing this exercise find that they start off with some conventional answer almost automatically, but when they have had some time to actually absorb the idea of being unable to fail, come up with an entirely different, and sometimes surprising, answer. Your answer will tell you what you really want to achieve.

And remember this…

It is not your fault.

It is not your fault!

IT IS NOT YOUR FAULT!

It is a set up.

We were set up.

Let that sink in…

The thing that is so important about the issue of Romantic Relationships is to realize how we were set up to fail in romance - to really get it on a gut level, so that we can forgive ourselves… and then begin to heal.

RESPONSIBILITY

Once we start letting go of feeling responsible for something we were powerless over, letting go of the false guilt and toxic shame about our mistakes and failures in romance, then we can start to learn how to take healthy risks.

First, consider this…

Although it is important to let go of feeling responsible for those things we were truly powerless over, we <u>must</u> take total responsibility for the entirety of our lives because the thing that makes the difference between a successful person and one who fails is the ability to take full responsibility.

For instance, if you started a business and it failed because your employees were not dependable or committed then you would be wise to acknowledge that you didn't have the management skills required to build a cohesive and dedicated team. But you can learn from the experience and, before you consider starting up another business venture, expand your knowledge about management and team building.

In other words, look for the silver-lining every time you get knocked off your path. Then pick yourself up and look for the lessons and opportunities. For instance:

* If you do not like the way you are feeling – no matter the reason – only you can change that. It is your life and your feelings. Blaming can be entertaining but is non-productive and a waste of time.

* Although loving and losing is painful it is likely much better than never loving at all. The more we heal our childhood emotional wounds and change the dysfunctional intellectual programming the clearer we can see reality.

* The more we learn to have boundaries, to ask for what we need, to be direct and honest in our communication, the healthier we become in our relationships. Healthy enough to get out of them quickly if we see too many warning signs.

Entering into a romantic relationships can be a great adventure if your perspective and expectations of them are realistic and healthy.

BE DESERVING OF ROMANTIC LOVE

If the foregoing information resonates with you it is important that you learn how to heal some of your wounds and forgive yourself enough to start owning up to the truth that you do deserve to have a loving relationship in your life.

Let that sink in…

You do deserve to have a loving relationship in your life.

Romantic Relationships are one of the most important arenas of spiritual growth available to us - it is important to our souls to be willing to take the risk of loving and losing. The gift of touch is an incredibly wonderful gift. One of the reasons we are here is to touch each other physically as well as spiritually, emotionally, and mentally.

Touch is not bad or shameful.

Our creator did not give us sensual and sexual sensations that feel so wonderful just to set us up to fail some perverted, sadistic life test.

Any concept of God that includes the belief that the flesh and the spirit cannot be integrated, that we will be punished for honoring our powerful human desires and needs, is rather harsh and will explain why some zealots are cold and unlovable.

Then there are those people who believe that the males of the species are genetically programmed to go around wanting to couple indiscriminately – those folks prefer to call it rape – with females of the species while females of the species are genetically programmed to want to bond to one man to produce children and then to protect and provide for her and her children.

That is genetic programming that is thousands of years out of date and unnecessary.

It seems we are set up by outmoded genetic programming - on top of our cultural dysfunctional programming. If so, we are set up to fail to get our needs met in Romantic Relationships in the same way that we are set up to fail in life - by being taught false beliefs about who we are and why we are here in human body, and false beliefs about the meaning and purpose of this dance of life.

The issue of how we are set up to fail to get our needs met in Romantic Relationships is complex - multi-leveled, multi-faceted, and multi-dimensional. But, the good news is that implementing our Dynamic Discovery process will allow you to "eat" your problems by simply taking it one small bite at a time... like eating an elephant... like taking the first step toward walking a thousand miles.

This dance of Codependence is a dance of dysfunctional relationships - of relationships that do not work to meet our needs. That does not mean just romantic relationships, or family relationships, or even human relationships in general. The fact that dysfunction exists in our romantic, family, and human relationships is a symptom of the dysfunction that exists in our relationship with life - with being human. It is a symptom of the dysfunction which exists in our relationships with ourselves as human beings.

The dysfunction that exists in our relationship with ourselves is a symptom of Spiritual depletion, of not being in balance and harmony with the universe, of feeling disconnected from our Spiritual source. That is why it is so important to enlarge our perspective. To look beyond the romantic relationship in which we are having problems. To look beyond the dysfunction that exists in our relationships with other people. The more we enlarge our perspective, the closer we get to the cause instead of just dealing with the symptoms. For example, the more we look at the dysfunction in our relationship with ourselves as human beings the more we can understand the dysfunction in our romantic relationships.

HEALTHY RELATIONSHIPS
(ARE INTERDEPENDENT, NOT CODEPENDENT)

You may find your prince or princess but they will have their own issues to deal with, so it is unlikely that you are going to live happily-ever-after. Relationships need work, not some magic wand that makes everybody happy. Every life has some ups and downs but there is a way to be mostly content and happy within yourself – but only if you can shed your codependent inclinations.

A healthy romantic relationship is based on interdependence. Codependence and interdependence are two very different dynamics. Codependence is about giving away power over our self-esteem. Interdependence is about making allies, forming partnerships. It is about forming connections with other beings. Interdependence means that we give someone else some power over our welfare and our feelings.

It is impossible to love without giving away some power.

When we choose to love someone or something (a person, a pet, a car, etc.) we are giving them the power to make us happy, and we cannot do that without also giving them the power to hurt us or cause us to feel angry or scared.

One of the false beliefs that it is important to let go of is the belief that we need another person in our lives to make us whole. As long as we believe that someone else has the power to make us happy then we are setting ourselves up to be victims. Wanting is entirely different from needing.

Let me explain…

Human wants are the things human beings desire for themselves. Wants come after all the human needs have been accomplished. Human wants always appear when people are idle and want to fill that idle time.

If the item is necessary for your survival, it is a need. This includes things such as basic shelter, clothing, food and water. Ask yourself if the "thing" is necessary for reasonable living. You may not 'need' something to survive, but you may need it in order to maintain a basic living setup.

However, in North America, for example, the definition of need will no doubt differ from that in a third world country. For instance, you don't need to take a shower to survive, but most of us consider that necessary. You don't need electricity, but most would consider it as such. You may not need a car to get to work, but you most likely need transportation of some kind. You may not need the latest fashions for your work clothes, but you probably need a few clothing items that are suitable for work. But entertainment, extra food beyond what you need and more clothing than you need, cable TV, Internet and other luxuries, on the other hand, are probably wants.

Learn the definition of a want in your life, bearing in mind that a want is basically something you have a strong desire for but isn't necessary for maintaining life. The place you live probably requires that you pay for utilities such as electricity, water, gas, trash and sewerage. While these aren't strictly necessary for survival, they most likely fall into the need category.

If you remember, on page 6 our Five Basic Human Needs were described thusly:

> In psychology, it is assumed that people have certain basic needs and in our Dynamic Discovery program they are classified under five headings for which we apply the acronym LAFFS:
>
> 1) **Love & Belonging** - this includes sex, families or loved ones as well as groups.
>
> 2) **Achievement, Power and Recognition** - which includes feeling worthwhile as well as winning.
>
> 3) **Freedom** - includes independence, autonomy, your own 'space'.
>
> 4) **Fun** - includes pleasure and enjoyment.
>
> 5) **Survival** - includes nourishment and shelter,

More About Codependency

One of the first steps to opening up to the possibility of having a healthy relationship is to start changing the dysfunctional attitudes and beliefs we learned in childhood. Our attitudes, beliefs, and definitions set up our expectations and perspectives which in turn dictate our emotional relationships. In order to change our relationship patterns we need to change the attitudes and beliefs so that we will stop expecting the magic of fairy tales in our romantic relationships.

Take note of this …

A healthy romantic relationship is based on interdependence.

Taking our self-definition and self-worth from outside or external sources is dysfunctional because it causes us to give power over how we feel about ourselves to people and forces which we cannot control. If your self-esteem is based on people, places, and things; money, property, and prestige; looks, talent, intelligence; then you are set up to be a victim. People will not always do what you want them to; property can be destroyed by an earthquake or flood or fire; money can disappear in a stock market crash or bad investment; looks will change as you get older. Everything changes. All outside or external conditions are temporary.

We are Spiritual beings having a human experience - our worth as beings is not dependent upon any outer or external condition. As Spiritual beings, we long for unconditional love – and it's likely we always will. It's only through owning the truth of who we really are and integrating it into our relationship with ourselves that we can really enjoy our human experiences. And it's then that we start becoming interdependent and begin to give power away in conscious, healthy ways - because our self-worth is no longer dependent on outside sources.

In order to live we need to be interdependent. We cannot participate in life without giving away some power over our feelings and our welfare – and this is not just about people. If we put money in a bank we are giving some power over our feelings and welfare to that bank. If we have a car we have a dependence on it and will have feelings if something happens to it. If we live in society we have to be interdependent to some extent and give some power away. The key is to be conscious in our choices and own responsibility for the consequences. The way to healthy interdependence is to be able to see things clearly - to see people, situations, life dynamics and most of all ourselves clearly. If we are not working on healing our childhood wounds and changing our childhood programming then we cannot begin to see ourselves clearly let alone anything else in life.

Being a Codependent person causes us to keep repeating patterns that are familiar. So we pick untrustworthy people to trust, undependable people to depend on, unavailable people to love. By healing our emotional wounds and changing our intellectual programming we can start to practice discernment in our choices so that we can change our patterns and learn to trust ourselves. As we develop healthy self-esteem – as is detailed in our e-book, Dynamic Discovery – then we can consciously take the risk of loving, of being interdependent, without buying into the belief that the behavior of others determines our self-worth. We will have feelings - we will get hurt, we will be scared, we will get angry - because those feelings are human emotions. Feelings are a part of our total behavior system that, along with physiology, is driven by our thoughts and actions. By changing our intellectual paradigm - our attitudes, beliefs, and definitions - we can stop expecting life to be something it is not.

We humans approach any task – whether it is to manage our weight, our retirement account, or anything else– with mental models that reflect the world as we understand it. We create these models out of our prior experience and whatever knowledge we have (real or imaginary, naive or sophisticated). Once formed, mental models are all important because they determine not only how we make sense of the world, but also how we act and what strategies we use to achieve our goals.

We can stop expecting relationships to be magic just because falling in love feels magical. We can start having a realistic view of relationships which will allow us to be responsible enough to do the work it takes to work through issues, to keep communication happening, to form a healthy interdependent partnership with another human being. It is in taking responsibility and working through issues that the true magic of emotional intimacy can flower. The sacred magic that is love is worth the effort.

Two people consciously working together can be a very beautiful experience.

COMMUNICATION IS KEY

The single most important component in a healthy relationship is the ability to communicate. If two people have the capacity to communicate with each other, then any issue can be worked through to some kind of clarity.

In terms of surface communication, it is very important to establish a common language where the words both partners use have the same meaning because misunderstandings and arguments come from different interpretations of various words due to a variety of factors – that is, they were raised in different geographic, religious, or cultural environments, have different educational or economic levels, different life experiences, etc. Two people who are on Spiritual paths might speak a slightly different language because one has been involved in Twelve Step Recovery while another has been pursuing a cultural or religious path.

Let's divide communication into two levels: surface communication having to do with ideas, facts, details, concepts, etc., and emotional communication. In reality, of course, all communication contains aspects of both levels - and in a Romantic Relationship, the emotional level is by far the most important and most difficult.

It is very important, right from the beginning of the relationship to strive for clarity in communication. The single most useful tool is simply to ask. You might ask, "How do you define that word?" or "What did you just hear me say?" Very often, you will find that what the other person heard was not what you were attempting to convey.

And that can open another opportunity for learning in order to communicate better.

Listening is also important. In order to truly listen it is necessary to be fully and consciously present - and the difficulty with being present is caused by unhealed emotional wounds. If we are not able to be emotionally honest with ourselves then it is impossible to be present and comfortable in our own skins in the moment. Obviously then, we are also incapable of being present with, and emotionally honest with, others.

In terms of the emotional level of communication, there are many aspects to consider. A symptomatic aspect is something that may seem simple but is actually one that relatively few of us have mastered; the ability to listen. In order to truly listen it is necessary to be present - and the difficulty with being present is caused by unhealed emotional wounds.

If we are not able to be emotionally honest with ourselves then it is impossible to be present and comfortable in our own skins in the moment. Obviously then, we are also incapable of being present with, and emotionally honest with, others. Listening is far more than just the absence of talking or the appearance of paying attention. Listening involves more than just hearing the words that another person is saying. In order to truly hear what another person is attempting to communicate, it is necessary to be tuned in to what is going on underneath the words.

Communication is only partly about content - just as important in communication are things like body language, eye contact, underlying emotional currents. When we are present in our bodies in the moment and paying attention it is easy to discern if the other person is really talking to us - as opposed to talking at us, or telling a story. In the beginning of any relationship, people tell each other stories about their past - it is part of getting to know each other. What is important is to be able to be present while telling the story. That involves not just the other person but also ourselves. Being present starts with being conscious of ourselves - it involves listening and paying attention to ourselves and our end of the communication.

If I am listening to myself while telling someone a story about my past, I can catch myself when I get to a part of the story that I have creatively embellished over the years. As we learn and grow, our perspective of our past changes and it is very important to be able to listen to ourselves so that we can catch ourselves in places where we have exaggerated or rationalized something from our past. One of the important parts of the healing process is telling our story - and if we just regurgitate an old tape by rote we are not being present and paying attention. If we have the capacity to be present with ourselves while telling our story, that means we also have the capacity to be present with the other person.

You could be in the middle of telling a story and see in the other persons eyes that they aren't listening - which gives you the opportunity to stop and ask what is going on. If you are not present enough to see the other person isn't listening then you are just talking at that person. And conversely, you will be able to recognize when that person is talking at you.

Communication involves being able to talk to and listen to others - the ability to be present in our bodies in the moment

EMOTIONAL HONESTY IS NECESSARY

Anyone who is unconscious to how the people and events of their past have shaped who they are today, is incapable of being present in the now and having a healthy relationship. When we are reacting unconsciously to the emotional wounds and old tapes from our childhoods, we are being emotionally dishonest in the moment, we are mostly reacting to how we felt in a similar dynamic in the past, not clearly responding to what is happening in the present.

Codependence is an emotional defense system that tries to take ego credit for things that go the way we want them to, and blames someone else when they do not. If you have not been working on healing your emotional wounds, then any feedback will be felt as criticism - as being wrong or bad - and your defense system reacts by becoming defensive.

Once you learn how to intervene in your own process so that you are not living life in reaction to old wounds then you will start being capable of having healthy emotional intimacy.

If you are in a relationship, check it out the next time you have a fight: Maybe you are both acting like you did when you were twelve-year-olds. If you are a parent, maybe the reason you have a problem sometimes is because you are reacting to your six-year-old child out of your six-year-old behaviors. If you have a problem with Romantic Relationships maybe it is because your fifteen-year-old self is picking your mates for you. If you are reacting out of what your emotional truth was when you were five or nine or fourteen, then you are not capable of responding appropriately to what is happening in the moment; you are not being in the present. When you are reacting out of your childhood emotional wounds, then what you are feeling may have very little to do with the situation you are in or with the people with whom you are dealing in the moment. In order to "be" in the moment in a healthy, age-appropriate way it is necessary to heal your inner child – yeah, that one. The inner child you have heard so much about, the one you alternately want to kick in the rump and then want to cuddle and coddle. The inner child you need to heal is actually your inner child who has been running your life because you have been unconsciously reacting to life out of the emotional wounds and attitudes, the old tapes, of your childhood.

Running the present from your past is not a really good approach to happiness.

The single biggest problem with most relationships is that there are too many people involved. A Romantic Relationship is supposed to be two people in partnership sharing of who they are, sharing their hearts, minds, bodies, and souls with each other. Anyone who has not done their emotional healing is bringing a plethora of people into any relationship they get involved in. Some of these people include:

- Parents, siblings, relatives; ministers, teachers, the junior high school bully.

- Everyone that they have ever had a romantic relationship with.

- The Prince and Princess of fairy tales, the lyrics of songs, and the characters from books and movies.

Just to think of how many ghosts are in the room, when two unconscious people are interacting, is mind boggling. Anyone who is unconscious to how the people and events of their past have shaped who they are today, is incapable of being present in the now and having a healthy relationship. When we are reacting unconsciously to the emotional wounds and old tapes from our childhoods, we are being emotionally dishonest in the moment - we are mostly reacting to how we felt in a similar dynamic in the past, not clearly responding to what is happening in the present.

Pay attention to this…

We all learned to see life and self from a dysfunctional perspective - from a perspective that taught us it was shameful to be bad or wrong. We learned to blame. Since the perspective of life which civilization is founded upon is black and white, right and wrong - we got the message that if we could not figure out how to blame someone else, then it must be our fault. Toxic shame is the feeling that I am somehow defective, that there is something wrong with who I am as a being. That feeling of being defective is so painful that we are willing to do almost anything to avoid sinking into that abyss of pain within.

So we blame someone or something outside of ourselves to protect our self. A dysfunctional civilization which teaches us to look outside for our self-worth, also teaches us to look outside for a villain. Those who believe that the best defense is a good offense, will attack by pointing out where the other person is wrong or bad. When confronted we blame. We either blame the other or we blame ourselves - in which case we sink into depression and despair, into abusing alcohol, drugs, food, etc.

This is the reason that most relationships turn into power struggles about who is right and who is wrong. Who has more right to feel victimized by the other? We come up with whatever justification and rationalization we can to deflect the blame from ourselves - as a way of self preservation. These behaviors are not bad or shameful; they are the inevitable dynamic set up when two people, who have not healed their emotional wounds and changed their dysfunctional programming, interact. We are powerless over the dynamic until we start becoming co-creators of our life by healing the past so that it is not dictating our life today. It is impossible to truly hear what another person is saying when we are busy loading up the big guns for our counterattack. We cannot be present in the moment if our emotional defenses are triggered by what is happening now. And these triggers can be a tone of voice, a gesture (pointing a finger), a word or phrase, almost anything. When old wounds are gouged we are pulled out of the now and into our feelings from the past.

Managing the present from the long-ago past. What fun! And what a waste of time and effort.

Once we start learning how to recognize when we are reacting and being defensive, then we can start getting more emotionally honest - with our self and with others. When we learn how to intervene in our own process so that we are not living life in reaction to old wounds then we start being capable of having healthy emotional intimacy. When two people are both working on their healing there is a possibility of communication and emotional honesty. The more we heal the past, the fewer people are intruding on our relationship in the moment. Those people - our parents or past romantic partners - will still be in our psyche but we will be conscious enough to recognize them when they start invading the now. Then we can communicate what we are learning about our self from our reactions to our partner and share our pain and fear and anger and sadness with her/him.

Now that is true emotional intimacy.

CHANGE

Life is constantly changing. There are always going to be endings and new beginnings. There is always going to be grief and pain and anger about what we have to let go of, and fear of what is to come. It is not because we are bad or wrong or shameful. It is just the way the game works. So there is good news and bad news. The bad news is that it's a stupid game - or at least it feels like it some of the time. The good news is that there are new tools to help us learn how to change our behaviors so as to find a way to comfort, confidence and happiness.

Let that sink in…

Changing one or more behaviors can open the door to comfort, confidence and happiness.

In Dynamic Discovery we learn that the rules of the game of life – the rules we have been playing by for thousands of years – really don't work anymore. If they ever did. We also learn that we can create our own rules from which to manage our own life… as long as our own rules are based on the Best Interest concept.

Think about it:

- How can you get into trouble if your every act is filtered through the Best Interest concept?

- The more you understand the Best Interest concept the easier it becomes to nurture yourself by not shaming and judging yourself.

- The more you understand the Best Interest concept the easier it becomes to accept the concept of unconditional love – and unconditional love does not mean being a doormat but starts with loving yourself enough to protect yourself from people you love if that is necessary.

Let that sink in...

Sometimes it is necessary to protect yourself from people you love, if those people are still stuck in their dysfunctional lifestyle.

THE EMOTIONAL DYNAMICS OF DYSFUNCTIONAL ROMANTIC RELATIONSHIPS

The way the dynamic in a dysfunctional relationship works is on a come-here-go-away cycle. When one person is available the other tends to pull away. If the first person becomes unavailable the other comes back and pleads to be let back in. When the first becomes available again then the other eventually starts pulling away again. It happens because our relationship with self is not healed. As long as I don't love myself then there must be something wrong with someone who loves me - if someone doesn't love me than I have to prove I am worthy by winning that person back. On some level we are trying to earn the love of our unavailable parent to prove to ourselves that we are worthy and lovable.

Here is a classic codependent scenario: one partner is asked where they want to eat and reply, "Oh, I don't care, wherever you want to," and then being angry because they are taken somewhere they don't like. This is a (not unusual) case where one partner thinks the other partner should be able to read their mind and know what they want to do. Typically, in relationships, one partner will ask the other to do something and the person who can't say I don't want to do that, will agree to do it and then not do it. This will result in nagging and scolding which will cause more anger and passive-aggressive behavior. And the war is on!

Passive-aggressive behavior can take the form of sarcasm, procrastination, chronic lateness, being a party pooper, constantly complaining, being negative, offering opinions and advice that is not asked for, being the martyr, slinging arrows (whatever have you done to your hair, gained a little weight haven't we?), etc.

Conflict is an inherent part of relationships and is to be worked through to grow from - conflict is an important part of the garden that grows deeper intimacy.

It is normal for relationships in this society to deteriorate into power struggles over who is right and who is wrong.

PASSIVE AND AGGRESSIVE

The Aggressive-Aggressive defense is called the militant bulldozer. This person, basically the counterdependent, is the one whose attitude is "I don't care what anyone thinks." This is someone who will run you down and then tell you that you deserved it. This is the survival of the fittest, hard-driving capitalist, self-righteous religious fanatic, who feels superior to most everyone else in the world. This type of person despises the human weakness in others because he/she is so terrified and ashamed of her/his own humanity.

The Aggressive-Passive person, or self-sacrificing bulldozer, will run you down and then tell you that they did it for your own good and that it hurt them more than it did you. These are the types of people who aggressively try to control you for your own good - because they think that they know what is right and what you should do and they feel obligated to inform you. This person is constantly setting him/herself up to be the perpetrator because other people do not do things the right way, that is, his/her way.

The Passive-Aggressive, or militant martyr, is the person who smiles sweetly while cutting you to pieces emotionally with her/his innocent sounding, double-edged sword of a tongue. These people try to control you for your own good but do it in more covert, passive-aggressive ways. They only want the best for you, and sabotage you every chance they get. They see themselves as wonderful people who are continually and unfairly being victimized by ungrateful loved ones - and this victimization is their main topic of conversation/focus in life because they are so self-absorbed that they are almost incapable of hearing what other people are saying.

The Passive-Passive, or self-sacrificing martyr, is the person who spends so much time and energy demeaning him/herself, and projecting the image that he/she is emotionally fragile, that anyone who even thinks of getting mad at this person feels guilty. They have incredibly accurate, long-range, stealth guilt torpedoes that are effective even long after their death. Guilt is to the self-sacrificing martyr what stink is to a skunk: the primary defense. These are all defense systems adopted out of a necessity to survive. They are all defensive disguises whose purpose is to protect the wounded, terrified child within.

These are broad general categories, and individually we can combine various degrees and combinations of these types of behavioral defenses in order to protect ourselves.

Passive-aggressive behavior is the expression of anger indirectly. This happens because we got the message one way or another in childhood that it was not okay to express anger. Since anger is energy that cannot be completely repressed it gets expressed in indirect ways. This takes the form one way or another, overtly or subtly, of us acting out the Codependent battle cry: "I'll show you! I'll get me ..."

COUNTERDEPENDENCY

The expanded usage of the term Codependent now includes counterdependent behavior. We have come to understand that both the passive and the aggressive behavioral defense systems are reactions to the same kinds of childhood trauma, to the same kinds of emotional wounds.

Counterdependents are people who take a position in relationships to ensure they are not dependent on others for emotional security, status, etc.

Within the family system, children adopt certain roles according to their family dynamics. Some of these roles are more passive, some are more aggressive, because in the competition for attention and validation within a family system the children must adopt different types of behaviors in order to feel like an individual. A large part of what we identify as our personality is in fact a distorted view of who we really are due to the type of behavioral defenses we adopted to fit the role or roles we were forced to assume according to the dynamics of our family system. Each of us has our own spectrum of behavioral defenses to protect us from fear of intimacy.

We can be codependent in one relationship and counterdependent in another - or we can swing from codependent to counterdependent within the same relationship.

Also, it is interesting to note that Dr. Nicholas Jenner – a counseling psychologist with a specialty in Cognitive Behavioral Therapy techniques – states that codependency, when left to fester, can turn into counter-dependency.

How very confusing.

To some degree it is healthy to seek to be emotionally independent of others but this needs to be balanced with the ability to be appropriately engaged with others.

Where the habit of maintaining emotional distance predominates, this can be associated with and cause mental health and behavioral difficulties. Where counter-dependency is the state of refusal of attachment, the denial of personal need and dependency, and narcissistic tendencies become the default attitudes.

Taken to an extreme, counter-dependent people can reach the point where their self-identity arises from their acts of opposition and defiance and their behavior can be very disruptive, making it difficult for them to hold down jobs or maintain relationships of any kind.

Such behavior patterns are thought to result from a deep-seated fear of intimacy.

Let's review this problem…

- The Counterdependent is the opposite of the Codependent.
- The Counterdependent has experienced a repeated failure of the significant persons in his life being trustworthy.
- Chronic and repeated violation of trust by a child sets in motion an inability to trust (without cause) the close and important persons in the Counterdependents life i.e. girlfriend, wife, parent, etc.
- As a child he may have experienced chronic hurt because the adults in his life failed to function responsibly.

If you can identify with the following symptomology, you are likely counterdependent:

- believe that you don't need anything from anyone.
- trust no one but yourself.
- find it hard to feel close to anyone, even wife and children.
- use violence or the threat of violence to force getting your way.
- maintain a relationship only with persons who don't demand a lot of closeness from you.
- resist making any commitments in a relationship.
- resist asking for or showing that you need help.
- be out of touch with the depth of your feelings.
- deny your feelings to others.
- resist showing affection.
- not like touching or hugging.

Remember, most of these issues begin in childhood and are deeply ingrained in our psyche. Change won't happen by accident. You are not crazy, you can recover if you're willing to do the work – and our Dynamic Discovery program works well with these types of problems.

For details on Dynamic Discovery, see our website www.DynamicDiscovery.ca.

CONCLUSION

Making one or more behavior changes is usually a process, not necessarily a single event. Long-term behavior change changes our way of living, the way we feel, and our mental attitude. Because you are reading this you may already have started the process of change, which probably began with the realization, or just a suspicion, that your relationship with your partner or significant other was not progressing in a way that was either satisfying or healthy.

The knowing or suspicion that something was amiss was likely what drew you to us – and we are pleased and flattered that you chose Dynamic Discovery. Using our program as your vehicle for change is obviously voluntary and, for the most part, it is learning to live life from a new and different point of view. The challenge is to be patient while you are absorbing your new skills and to experiment with different points of view in new and creative ways.

True freedom is when we let go of the pain and fear that is part of unhappiness and, as we let go, happiness, freedom and joy become a way of life, rather than just words spoken or read. I have seen that happen again and again. Joy and love of life is the reward for walking through the 'pain' of growth.

Just as a map is not the territory but a guide to the territory, I hope that this book will prove to be a map to the territory of your most important relationship.

The amount of happiness that is available to you as you continue to apply your newfound skills and techniques is infinite because you define the goal and there is no limit to the passion and meaning that you can derive from your journey. You can incorporate any existing tool or program within the larger context of this journey as long as it makes you more aware, awake and responsible. And that is what a pathway to freedom is for.

Because your path is right there for you, I want you to remember that, no matter what happens, the path that you created is right before you and all you have to do is walk that path and feel the power of your design.

I'd like to offer you an ally in this process which will prove to be helpful to you. Have you read Napoleon Hill's 'Philosophy of Achievement' books? Hill was a prolific writer, producing some 30 volumes and all with a consistent message: Success.

The truly amazing thing is that Hill's first book was written in 1925, is still available today, and has sold over 20 million copies.

Hill considered freedom, democracy, capitalism, and harmony to be important contributing elements to this philosophy. Hill claimed throughout his writings that without these foundations upon which to build, successful personal achievements were not possible. He contrasted his philosophy with others' and thought that the Achievement Philosophy was superior. He felt that it was responsible for the success Americans enjoyed for the better part of two centuries. Negative emotions such as fear, selfishness, etc., had no part to play in his philosophy. Hill considered those emotions to be the source of failure for unsuccessful people Hill tantalized his readers by referring to the secret of success through analogy, such as: If you truly desire money so keenly that your desire is an obsession, you will have no difficulty in convincing yourself that you will acquire it. The object is to want money, and to be so determined to have it that you convince yourself that you will have it. However, you can never have riches in great quantities unless you work yourself into a white heat of desire for money, and actually believe you will possess it. Do not presume it is this which is the secret that Hill refers to, but the definition of the 'secret' is far more effective if realized by the reader when they are ready for it.

Napoleon Hill eventually resolved the secret at the end of his book 'The Law of Success'; it is the Golden Rule. Only by working harmoniously in co-operation with other individuals or groups of individuals and thus creating value and benefit for them will one create sustainable achievement for oneself.

You see, what Hill wanted to do to his readers and students — which I don't, of course, want to do to you — was to find some way of motivating them to be congruent and expressive in their behavior at all times and as creative as they could be as human beings. He wanted them to mobilize their resources so that each act that they performed would be a full representation of all the potential that was available to them — all the personal power that they had that was available to them at any moment in time.

Borrowing from 'The Teachings of don Juan' by Carlos Castenada, during their travels together Juan was educating Carlos about the realities of life. Specifically what Juan, a Yaqui Indian, told Carlos was "At any moment that you find yourself hesitating, or if at any moment you find yourself putting off until tomorrow trying some new piece of behavior that you could do today, or doing something you've done before, then all you need to do is glance over your left shoulder and there will be a fleeting shadow. That shadow represents your death, and at any moment it might step forward, place its hand on your shoulder and take you. So, that the act that you are presently engaged in might be your very last act and therefore fully representative of you as your last act on this planet."

One of the ways you can use this advice constructively is to understand that it is indulgent to hesitate. When you hesitate, you are acting as though you are immortal. You are not. You don't even know the place and the hour of your death.

And so one thing you can do – to remind yourself that not to bother to hesitate is not to act unprofessional – is to just suddenly glance over your left shoulder and remember that death is standing there, and make death your advisor. And know that he or she will always tell you to do something representative of your full potential as a person. You can afford no less.

Now, that's a little bit heavy. That's why I wouldn't tell that to you. But I will offer you an alternative: If at any point you discover yourself hesitating, or being incongruent, or putting off until tomorrow something you could try now, or just needing some new choices, or being bored, glance over your right shoulder and there I will be, urging you on. And reminding you that any questions you might have can be self-answered through the use of the magic question.

As a reminder, the magic question goes like this:

Suppose our meeting is over, you go home, do whatever you planned to do for the rest of the day. And then, sometime in the evening, you get tired and go to sleep. And in the middle of the night, when you are fast asleep, a miracle happens and all the problems that brought you here today are solved... just like that. But since the miracle happened overnight nobody is telling you that the miracle happened.

When you wake up the next morning, how are you going to start discovering that the miracle happened?

_____

_____

What else are you going to notice?

_____

_____

And that's just one way that your subconscious can make sense of, and deal with, all the material that it has absorbed during the Dynamic Discovery program.

Please note…

- Nothing in the world is a gift; whatever it is you have has been, in some way, worked for.

- Whatever there is to learn has to be learned the hard way.

- Turn the Dynamic Discovery concepts into a viable way of life by a process of repetition.

- Everything new in our lives, such as the Dynamic Discovery concepts, must be repeated to us to the point of exhaustion before we open ourselves to it.

ABOUT DYNAMIC DISCOVERY

When I think of the wasted dreams, the unfulfilled lives and the lost opportunities in so many of the people around me I feel sad... sad and more committed than ever to spreading the word about our Dynamic Discovery program. We can show you how to manage your Romantic Relationship... and much more as well because:

- Dynamic Discovery is a process of self-evaluation, based upon getting what <u>you</u> want and dealing <u>with</u> <u>your</u> needs and helping you to make effective and meaningful changes in your life through an innovative process for personal change.

- You will discover how to get started on getting what you really want from life, how to move from <u>unwanted</u> behaviors to <u>wanted</u> behaviors so as to regain control of your life and how to achieve balance in all aspects (mental / physical / spiritual). You will also discover how to improve your personal image and how to make gain <u>without</u> pain.

All you need to bring with you is an open-mind.

Check out our website at www.DynamicDiscovery.ca

RESOURCES

Credit for much of my base of knowledge belongs to:

* The Alandel School and Clinic (hypnotherapy training)

* The 20 years of experience I received while working as a counselor and employee assistance program manager for Bob Giles of Human Resources Services Ltd. (HRS)

* The Heartview Foundation of Mandan, North Dakota, where I learned about addictions

* 26 years of immersion in the program of Alcoholics Anonymous

* 25 years of studying various programs/approaches such as NLP, Psychology, Cognitive Behavioural Therapy, Quantum Physics and Reality Therapy.

* Abraham Maslow's hierarchy of needs

* Dr. William Glasser, a psychiatrist who developed Reality Therapy / Control Theory.

* The writings of Milton Erickson which drew upon his own experiences to provide examples of the power of the unconscious mind. He was largely self-taught.

* Dave Elman, who was self-taught and wrote "Hypnotherapy" which was self-published and is the definitive guide for hypnotherapy.

* The first 100 members of Alcoholics Anonymous who contributed to the development of the book Alcoholics Anonymous (generally known as The Big Book) and my friends from AA and Al-Anon.

* The teachings of Socrates, especially those concerning inductive reasoning (to draw logical conclusions) and his Four Principles of Philosophy.

* Tony Robbins - The Six Human Needs.

* Manfred Max-Neef (along with Antonio Elizalde and Martin Hopenhayn) developed the theory of Human Needs and Human-Scale Development.

www.ingramcontent.com/pod-product-compliance
Lightning Source LLC
Chambersburg PA
CBHW060650030426
42337CB00017B/2540